D1069053

CANDACE PARKER

PARKER

BASKETBALL STAR

by Shane Frederick

CAPSTONE PRESS
a capstone imprint

Stars of Sports is published by
Capstone Press, an imprint of Capstone
1710 Roe Crest Drive, North Mankato, Minnesota 56003
www.capstonepub.com

**Library of Congress Cataloging-in-Publication Data is available on
the Library of Congress website.**
ISBN: 9781543591767 (hardcover)
ISBN: 9781543591897 (eBook PDF)

Summary: When Candace Parker beat out all the boys at the McDonald's All-
American slam dunk contest in 2004, she became the first female player to win
the event. In the years that followed, Parker's list of achievements includes WNBA
Rookie of the Year, a two-time WNBA Most Valuable Player, and a two-time
Olympic Gold Medalist. Parker is also a mother, broadcaster, and role model.

Editorial Credits
Christianne Jones, editor; Ashlee Suker, designer; Eric Gohl, media researcher;
Laura Manthe, production specialist

Image Credits
Associated Press: Gus Ruelas, 5, Jim Mone, 27, Mark J. Terrill, 26, Miles Kennedy,
10, Wade Payne, 11; Newscom: Cal Sport Media/Anthony Nesmith, 24, Cal Sport
Media/Tim Gangloff, 15, Icon SMI/Darryl Dennis, 19, Icon SMI/Larry W. Smith,
9, Icon SMI/Randy Snyder, 13, Icon Sportswire/M. Anthony Nesmith, 28, Icon
Sportswire/Tony Quinn, cover, MCT/Harry E. Walker, 23, Reuters/Scott Audette,
14, Reuters/Sergio Perez, 21, SportsChrome/Ross Dettman, 6, ZUMA Press/Joseph
Garnett Jr., 16; Shutterstock: EFKS, 1, Featureflash Photo Agency, 25

Printed in the United States of America.
PA99

TABLE OF CONTENTS

Glossary terms are **BOLD** on first use.

SLAM DUNK

Candace Parker got loose on a **fast break**. She dribbled straight toward the basket. She jumped up and made history. With one hand on the ball, Parker dunked. The crowd went wild. It was only the second time a player had ever dunked in a Women's National Basketball Association (WNBA) game.

Parker had dunked in a game before. She did it in college at the University of Tennessee. She also did it in high school. But before Candace, there were not many females who sailed above the rim.

Parker throws down a dunk against the Indiana Fever. 〉〉〉

CHAPTER ONE

GOING UP

Candace Parker was born on April 19, 1986, in St. Louis, Missouri. When she was young, her family moved to Naperville, a city near Chicago. Parker's dad was a basketball player. So were her brothers. Her brother Anthony went on to play in the National Basketball Association (NBA). But Candace didn't play basketball at first. Her favorite sport was soccer.

When she reached eighth grade, Parker's family finally got her to try basketball. Her dad, Larry, was her first coach. Playing basketball quickly became her favorite thing to do. The sport came naturally, and Parker was always tall. In fact, she would grow to be 6 feet 4 inches tall. And she would become one of the best players in the country.

〈〈〈 Parker played basketball for Naperville Central High School.

HIGH SCHOOL DOMINATION

As a high school player, Parker **dominated**. She went to Naperville Central High School. In tenth grade, she became the first high school girl to slam dunk in a game. She was 15 years old. During her junior and senior seasons, Parker led her team to 68 wins and two losses. They won back-to-back state championships.

Each of those seasons, Parker sat out two games with a hurt knee. Those were the only games the Redhawks lost. After graduation, she won a slam dunk contest at a national high school all-star event. She beat boys and girls.

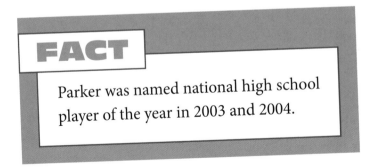

FACT

Parker was named national high school player of the year in 2003 and 2004.

In 2004, Parker was the star of the McDonald's All-American High School Basketball game.

〉〉〉

CHAPTER TWO
VOLUNTEER TIME

When she was a senior in high school, Parker had to make up her mind. Where would she go next? She agreed to play college basketball for coach Pat Summitt at the University of Tennessee. The Lady Volunteers were one of the best women's basketball teams in the country. They had won six national championships. Parker was going to help them win more.

>>> Coach Summitt prepares the Lady Volunteers for an upcoming game against Texas Tech.

<<< Parker and Coach Summitt talk during a game against Stanford.

"It's going to be fun to watch her develop and help take this game to a different level," Summitt said about Parker. "And you're going to see a player who is unique."

COLLEGE STAR

Parker didn't play her first year at Tennessee. She used that time to rest from a knee injury. Finally, she slipped on an orange Volunteers jersey. When she stepped onto the court for a game, she looked like a star. That season she slammed the first of seven dunks in her college career. She was the first woman to dunk twice in one game. She was also the first to dunk in a college **tournament** game.

Parker was named **Rookie** of the Year for the Southeastern Conference (SEC) that first season. She also hit the game-winning basket in the SEC tournament championship game. But there were bigger prizes ahead.

Parker brings the ball up court against Kentucky. 〉〉〉

Parker was a machine on **offense**. She reached 1,000 points faster than any Tennessee player ever had. It took just 56 games. At the end of her second season, the Lady Volunteers won their seventh national championship. Parker scored 17 points in the final game. She was named Most Valuable Player (MVP) of the Final Four.

〉〉〉 Parker hugs teammate Alex Fuller after Tennessee won the NCAA women's championship game in 2008.

In 2014, Parker became the sixth former Tennessee player to have her jersey retired.

The next season, Parker led the team to another national championship. She also won another MVP award. For the year, she **averaged** 21.3 points and 8.5 **rebounds** per game. After the season, she was named the best player in women's college basketball.

In three seasons for Tennessee, Parker scored 2,137 points. The team had a record of 101 wins and 10 losses. She could have gone back for one more year of college basketball. But Parker was ready for new challenges. After the 2008 NCAA championship game, she announced she was going to turn **professional**.

One day after the college season ended, the WNBA held its **draft** to choose players. The Los Angeles Sparks had the first pick. It was an easy choice. They picked the best player in the country: Candace Parker, the high-scoring superstar out of Tennessee. The WNBA's season is in the spring and summer, so Candace was off to California right away.

⟨⟨⟨ WNBA president Donna Orender poses with Parker after she was drafted by the Los Angeles Sparks.

THE SPARKS

The WNBA was just like college, just like high school, and just like eighth grade. Parker quickly became one of the best players on the court. During her first game with the Sparks, she scored 34 points and had 12 rebounds. As the season went on, she continued to out-score and out-rebound almost everybody. And, of course, she threw down a slam dunk.

Los Angeles had a record of 10 wins and 24 losses the season before Parker arrived. In Parker's first year, the Sparks were 20–14. She was named the WNBA's Rookie of the Year and the league's MVP.

She Does It All

In 2017, Candace Parker became the sixth player in WNBA history to record a triple-double. That means she reached double digits in points, rebounds, and assists in the same game. In 2018, Parker became the 20th player in WNBA history to score 5,000 career points.

⟩⟩⟩ Parker during the Sparks home opener in 2008

CHAPTER FOUR
GOOD AS GOLD

Candace Parker had an unbelievable year in 2008. She was a great player for the Tennessee Lady Volunteers and for the Los Angeles Sparks. But there was a third team that she helped lead to greatness.

In the summer of 2008, the WNBA took a break for the Summer Olympics. They were held in Beijing, China. Parker was part of Team USA. She wasn't the star of the team right away. She averaged 8.7 points per game going into the final against Australia. But with the gold medal in sight, Parker took over. She scored 14 points in the championship game. The United States won gold.

>>> Parker (left), Lisa Leslie (center), and Delisha Milton-Jones show off their Olympic gold medals.

FACT

Parker was named the Associated Press Female Athlete of the Year in 2008.

LONDON GOLD

Four years later, Team USA won gold again at the 2012 Olympics in London, England. Parker was one of the team leaders. She was third on the team in scoring. She was first in rebounds and blocked shots. In the gold-medal game against France, Parker scored 21 points and pulled down 11 rebounds.

The United States won its fifth Olympic championship in a row. Many thought Candace would make the Olympic team again in 2016. However, she didn't make the team. She was hurt and other WNBA stars had to step up.

World Traveler

When the WNBA season ends, many players move on to other professional leagues. Those leagues are located in different countries around the world. Parker played for a team in Russia, where she was also a star. She helped her team win five championships there. She has also played for teams in China and Turkey.

Parker leads a fast break during
an Olympic game against China. ⟩⟩⟩

CHAPTER FIVE

A CHAMPION AGAIN

After her first great season, Parker's playing time was limited over the next few years because she was hurt. In 2010, she averaged more than 20 points per game. But she was able to play in only 10 games. The next season, she was named to the WNBA All-Star Game for the first time. Parker couldn't play in the game, though, because of those injuries.

⟨⟨⟨ Parker at the 2013 WNBA All-Star Game

In 2012, Parker was healthy. She put together a strong, full season. She led the Sparks back to the playoffs. A year later, Parker was the best player in the WNBA again. She finally got to play in the All-Star Game. She scored 23 points and was named the game's Most Valuable Player. At the end of the 2013 season, she was named the league's MVP for the second time. There was just one thing missing—a WNBA championship.

TITLE TIME

Parker continued to be one of the WNBA's best players. In 2016, Parker and her teammates finally put together a championship run. The Sparks played the defending-champion Minnesota Lynx in the finals.

The series went the full five games. With the series tied 2–2, Candace scored 28 points and pulled down 12 rebounds in game five. The Sparks won 77–76.

》》》 Parker goes up against Rebekkah Brunson of the Minnesota Lynx in the WNBA finals.

》》》 The Sparks celebrate after winning the 2016 WNBA Championship.

"The journey to get here, I wouldn't have wanted to do it with anybody else," Candace said. "It's amazing, when you surround yourself with good people, how fun it is."

Candace **dedicated** the win to her college coach, Pat Summitt, who died earlier in the year.

LOOKING AHEAD

Candace Parker has taken women's basketball to new heights. It started with those slam dunks when she was a high school player. It's continued with college and professional championships and two Olympic gold medals.

Parker has begun working as a television **broadcaster**. She has announced women's and men's college games, as well as NBA games. But her spectacular playing career isn't over yet. Before it's done, she hopes to lead the Sparks to more championships.

TIMELINE

1986 born in St. Louis, Missouri

2003 leads Naperville High School to the Illinois state championship

2004 becomes the national high school player of the year for the second year in a row; leads Naperville to a second straight championship

2005 begins playing for the University of Tennessee

2007 takes the Lady Volunteers to the first of two straight NCAA championships

2008 is named national college player of the year; is picked number one in the WNBA draft by the Los Angeles Sparks; leads Team USA to a gold medal at the Olympics in Beijing, China; becomes WNBA Rookie of the Year and MVP

2012 wins another gold medal with Team USA at the Olympics in London, England

2013 receives a second WNBA MVP award

2016 wins an WNBA championship with the Sparks; named Finals MVP

GLOSSARY

AVERAGE (AV-uh-rij)—a player's total points, blocks, or rebounds in a season divided by the number of games played

BROADCASTER (BRAAD-ka-str)—a person who announces a program on radio or TV

DEDICATE (DED-uh-kate)—to honor someone you respect with one of your own achievements

DOMINATE (DAH-muh-nayt)—to control or rule over

DRAFT (draft)—the process of choosing a person to join a sports organization or team

FAST BREAK (fast brayk)— a quick play in which players outrun the defense to the basket

OFFENSE (aw-FENSS)—the team that is in control of the ball and is trying to score

PROFESSIONAL (pruh-FESH-uh-nuhl)—a level of a sport in which players get paid to play

REBOUND (REE-bound)—catching a ball that has missed the basket

ROOKIE (RUK-ee)—a player in his or her first year

TOURNAMENT (TUR-nuh-muhnt)—a series of matches between several players or teams, ending in one winner

READ MORE

Flynn, Brendan. *Superstars of the WNBA Finals.* North Mankato, MN: Abdo, 2018.

Ignotofsky, Rachel. *Women in Sports: 50 Fearless Athletes Who Played to Win.* Berkeley, CA: Ten Speed Press, 2017.

Mortensen, Lori. *Maya Moore: Basketball Star.* North Mankato, MN: Capstone Press, 2018.

INTERNET SITES

Candace Parker
www.candaceparker.com

WNBA
www.wnba.com

WNBA Facts for Kids
https://kids.kiddle.co/Women's_National_Basketball_Association

INDEX